The ABC's of Prospecting System

By

Dameon V. Russell

D & S Real Estate Education

The ABC's of Prospecting System

An advanced sales system; leads generation, CRM,
productivity enhancement, and
prospecting.

The ULTIMATE System for Every Real Estate Sales Professional!

2007 D & S Real Estate Education

A few positive thoughts.

"Just wanted to take a minute to thank you for the incredible information that you have shared with me and others enabling me to attain a success I thought would take years. Anyone who walks away from that seminar walks away with tons of information that can help them double, maybe triple their business, depending on what stage they are at and how much they want to apply what Dameon offers.

I've dealt with a few other real estate trainers, but nothing compares with Dameon's ABCs of Prospecting. The small investment I've made in his seminars has easily come back to me many, many times over. My production has almost tripled, my working hours are whittled down by a third, I am happier I am less stressed, I don't have to fight for the business."

If you care about your business, if you want to have a life, and if you want to have a business that doesn't depend totally on you , then you should be attending the seminar not only for the money that you're going to have. You just can't help but go up". Highly recommended for new agents, one year agents who have no clue how to market themselves. Price of the seminar is priceless....I fully endorse the ABC's of Prospecting seminar, Dameon Russell, and his method of teaching."

Best of luck
**Michael Chand, CENTURY 21® System
Realtor®, CENTURION® Top Producer.**

"I don't believe I have words to describe Dameon and what he has contributed to my success as a Realtor®.
All I could say is that Dameon has been the strongest link to my success. As a brand new agent, I closed 12 transactions within the first 7 months of my career - Thanks to my teacher, guide, mentor, and friend; Dameon."

Nooria Kakar, Realtor®
Agent of the Month (multiple)
CENTURY 21 Landmark Network

"Dameon's operational systems that he has put in place, are like nothing I have ever seen before. When I put his systems to work, I noticed a HUGE increase in my business. Dameon is in essence a teacher, and if you listen to what he has to say, and apply what he says to do, you and your career will go very far."

Steve Youmans, Realtor®
Career Development Specialist
CENTURY 21 Landmark Network

Author's note:
A good friend in the Industry coined a phrase which I feel is a direct parallel of the ABC's of Prospecting System; *"Plan your day, work your week, and visualize your month."*

George Sims, Sales Manager of Access Funding Mortgage coined that phrase. George is a venerable veteran of the Industry and is as innovative a marketer, manager and motivator as I have ever known.

CONTENTS

What You Should Know About D&S.

D&S Real Estate Education professional trainers have been responsible for creating several successful training programs and systems for real estate sales professionals.

Though our focus is primarily on the real estate sales professional, attendees of our seminars agree that the models, tools, and systems relayed indeed permeate through all facets of sales.

Our philosophy and core belief is that sales must begin with leads generation and that can only truly be achieved via direct, sustained warm contact conversion and management.

"You're either a lead generator, or a lead receiver; only the generators truly make it."

No matter the size of your sales business, success is dependent upon a few key functions and components; most real estate sales professionals overlook these components consistently.

The systems created and relayed by D&S facilitators are in direct address to these KEY components as we firmly believe and can evidence, that it is simply, how sales gets done!

Dameon V. Russell - Director, Business Development, CENTURY 21® Landmark Network

Mr. Russell began his real estate career over fifteen years ago in the business of Discounted Trust Deeds.

Over a four-year period he closed transactions totaling more than $61 million worth of loans encumbering real property in eleven states. Mr. Russell's knowledge of marketing and real estate is extensive and broad. His abilities in this regard are a function of excellent analytical and communicative skills.

Most applicable are his educational background in marketing strategies, his scope of knowledge in all aspects of the Real Estate Industry and implementation of stratagems relative to Business Development. Mr. Russell has a profound understanding of trends, and market diversities pertaining to all matters of real estate. More notable is his skill at converting such data to systematized strategy, and subsequently to revenue through structured integration and implementation.

He has created several successful real estate learning systems for Agent Career Development and delivers material in a focused easily followed manner, certain to never be dull. Mr. Russell has been a frequent Guest Lecturer on the subject of Marketing, at San Francisco State University, University of the Pacific, University of California Los Angeles and the University of Southern California.

For
Dominique Viana

It's important that you know up front that this book is not a sales "pep talk" or purely motivational narrative. This is a learning resource book – meaning – YOU WILL LEARN by reading this book! You will learn and gain insight into your business sufficient to elevate your business. In my delivery of the material I may seem occasionally intense (I do try to keep it somewhat light) but I take this very seriously, as should each of you.

This is your business, and in writing this book my objective has been to relay knowledge and a skill set VERY critical to that business. The fact that you acquired the book and have at least begun to read it, to me, clearly indicates that you place a high value on knowledge and are committed to your real estate sales business.

First of all let me impress upon you that you've made the right decision. You will close this book having completed it, a great deal wiser for having done so. The ABCs of Prospecting will hopefully remain with you as the primary operational system applied in your real estate sales business. Operational systems should be the skeleton or the frame upon which your business is built, operates, is sustained, and ultimately …..succeeds. As Business Development Director for a Century 21® System brokerage with 3 branches and a bit more than 100 active agents, part of my job was to devise, structure and implement operational systems both for the brokerage, and for the agents who look to the brokerage for support and guidance on the path to prosperity.

I've created such systems for transaction management, recruiting, an in-house call center/Client Services Center, and certainly marketing and personal promotion as well; but mainly for what I call ACD, (Agent Career Development). It's this "stuff", the "stuff" that ultimately makes a career; prospecting, CRM, and agent business models. I'm very proud of the ABCs of Prospecting system and I'm pleased to be able to bring it to you within this powerful resource book.

Oh yes, I did mention CRM didn't I? CRM is an acronym for one of the staples of real estate sales success; Client Relationship Management.

What you should also know is that Client Relationship Management is without question, the TRUE key to your success as a real estate sales professional. Well, you now know what it means, let me ask – are you actually diligently engaged in CRM efforts?

CRM is a substantial part of the ABCs of Prospecting system. Listen folks, when I say I create systems, usually that entails a thoughtful and strategic integration of several key components sequenced or bound together in a logical flow in order to exact a successful and efficient result. Now if you followed all of that, that's NOT to say that, I'm re-inventing the wheel. Listen I'm no more responsible for the sales genius behind CRM than Al Gore is for the invention of the internet!

CRM has been around, and frankly, has been the means by which successful sales gets done, well...... I'd wager since shortly after the Stone Age!

The ABCs of Prospecting system is made up of a few key components, each of individual importance to your real estate sales career, but collectively, WOW... just a remarkably POWERFUL combination. CRM for sure is one such component of the system. Another, of equal importance is database management.

Answer this question honestly; can you say you have or maintain a contacts database? How many contacts? Where do you have your database – Excel, Outlook, your PDA, post-its in a shoe box?

Now here's the million dollar question, what activities do you REGULARLY engage in with your database of contacts?

If I show you, truly show you, a sure fire way to work with your contacts, to convert cold contacts to warm, to derive substantial referrals from your database, to grow your database and thereby grow your business; would that, I wonder be worth the "price of admission"; figuratively speaking?

That is precisely what the ABC's of Prospecting System is designed to detail for you.

Let's get started!

LESSON ONE – The Magic Number

In terms of numbers, industry analysts as well as many Top Producers tell us the magic minimum number is 250; that is, in order to achieve benchmark levels of success as a real estate sales professional, you need to be managing, actively managing, 250 contacts in your database; 250 contacts. You tell me you have anything less, in any market but especially in tighter market conditions, and I say, well... it's a start, but you need to improve upon that.

Now, that's not to say that in order to make money you must have 250 contacts, or that you shouldn't aspire to have more. What it does tell you is that your database IS your business.... as it grows, your business grows. If your database growth is stagnant, well... so goes your business.

Bottom line, a database of 250 contacts represents a moderate sized real estate sales business; one with significant earning and growth potential. Regardless of how many contacts you currently have, you need to establish a growth pace of 15 to 25 added contacts per week; every week! ......15 to 25 added contacts per week; every week! But remember, your contacts database is ONLY as beneficial as you make it. Fail to execute and sustain a diligent CRM effort, and you will almost certainly fail, regardless of the size of your database.

I ask real estate agents of various years this question; what do you believe your job to be, meaning as a real estate sales professional, what do you believe your primary function each day to be?

Without any doubt I can tell you that the answers I most commonly get to that question are something in the realm of, "to help people realize their dreams of home ownership", "to help clients buy/sell or transact in real estate". Good answers; but neither is the right answer! This is not the job or primary function of a real estate sales person; but rather a bi-product of successfully doing your actual job!

As an agent in this business, your job is to get up each morning, go out into the world, and meet people. That's it. Of course there's a bit more to the gig, but this is your primary role. Do it faithfully, diligently, successfully and you will certainly have your share of people to help transact in real estate. Listen, this is NOT rocket science; it's called prospecting and if you're not doing it, or don't have a solid plan to do so consistently, you will not be able to sustain any sort of growth, nor your business in general.

You're either a leads generator, or a leads receiver.

Think about that for a second; you're either in the leads generation business, or you're not going to BE in business, not for too long anyway, especially in tighter market conditions. Do you TRULY want to be more successful in your real estate sales career? You are reading this book so I assume so. In that case, you best understand that you are NOT in the real estate business – you are in the leads generation business! You MUST come to terms with that reality immediately.

That number, 250, 250 contacts; what does it really mean? I want to convey in this Lesson that simply having a database of 250 contacts does not automatically equate to, or beget success as a real estate sales professional. It is the management of those contacts that brings about success. I know many moderate producing sales agents with more than 250 contacts. Their production level is merely moderate because they have no system to facilitate the management of those contacts. The conversion processes necessary to systematically convert contacts to transactions is not in place. Likewise, I know several agents who are actively managing their database yet their production is lacking because the number of contacts they have is minimal. In his fantastic book, *Millionaire Real Estate Agent*, Gary Keller refers frequently to the three "L's" of the Millionaire Real Estate Agent; *Listings*, *Leads*, and *Leverage*. The ABC's of Prospecting System is designed to facilitate leads generation. However, its most powerful contribution to your career will be the leverage it provides as an operational system enabling you to successfully, diligently, and consistently manage greater numbers of contacts. In doing so, the system ensures that you will be able to continue to grow your business, beyond even your most ambitious aspirations.

LESSON TWO – Ready, Set ....Prospect!

Now you're ready for PROSPECTING!

The true beauty of prospecting is found in its simplicity. The science, or if you prefer, the art, of prospecting requires a plan of action. Certainly, it's all about meeting and greeting at the core. Yet it does involve a bit of marketing, and self promotion, with quite a bit of necessary follow through, and follow-up.

The operational objective of prospecting is to "feed" your contacts database. A goal is required. I recommend a goal of 15 to 25. That is, you want to add 15 to 25 new contacts to your contacts database per week. This is very doable. As I stated earlier, the magic minimum number is 250. A minimum of 250 total contacts in your database, this can, but need not necessarily include your S.O.I., (sphere of influence). If you already have eclipsed this number, your goal should still be database growth of 15 to 25 new contacts per week.

Many agents I have coached invariably ask the question; "how do I add 15 to 25 people to my database every week?" Well, for those agents who may not be there mentally already, this type of prospecting success requires a shift in thinking.

One of my favorite movies consists of this very theme with regard to the primary character. The movie is *Romeo is Bleeding*, starring Gary Oldman, Lena Olin, and Roy Schieder; if you haven't seen it, I recommend it highly. The main character, played by Gary Oldman is a police officer, a Detective in fact. Oldman's character is a "dirty cop". Nothing major, he's actually a good guy in certain respects, he just gets in way over his head with the local mob boss, played by Schieder, and misplaces his trust in an infamous mob assassin played by Lena Olin. Anyway, Oldman's character, unbeknownst to his sweet wife, has a hole covered by an iron grate in the backyard of the couple's modest urban brownstone. In this hole he keeps all the cash; his ill gotten gains. In a very charming way he speaks to the hole, he actually dances out of pure joy as he makes deposits into the hole. Viewers have to imagine that the joy is born of his thoughts of an ever-growing nest egg.

The connection I make here to prospecting is brought about by the driving, motivational utterance frequently repeated by Oldman's character; "feed the hole, feed the hole, feed the hole." I consistently tell agents I coach that for them, their database is that hole and in order to bring about the necessary shift in thinking, they need to keep the driving phrase in their minds everyday; feed the hole, feed the hole, feed the hole!

The obvious point is that if you go about your day constantly mindful of the need to "feed the hole", you will in fact, do just that!

You "feed" your database by engaging persons you have contact with in your daily affairs. Simple conversations, communicate with people. This is sales, to some degree you must be an outwardly, open and engaging person. Many agents diligently do this, handing out an average of 10 business cards per day. That's good, it's very good; however these agents are failing themselves and their business in one essential respect. They are not getting anything in return.

At the grocery store, the bank, or perhaps dropping off the kids at school these agents will engage a person in conversation, the discussion turns toward real estate, the market, real estate finance and out comes the business card. As I said, this is good, this is precisely what you want to be doing daily. The problem is that most agents end that conversation with the good intentioned, "hey, it's been a pleasure speaking with you; please don't hesitate to give me call should you ever have the need."

You're running a business, business cards cost money, right? Where's the return on investment for that card? Sounds insignificant I know, but you must begin to look at your business in this manner. The return you're looking for in this case is the prospect's contact information!

"Feed the hole," bring the prospect's contact information back to the contacts database. This is how you grow your database; this is how you grow your business. How about this alternate ending; "hey, it's been wonderful speaking with you Andrew. It sounds like as a homeowner you really try to stay informed. I send out a market newsletter every month via email, let me get your email address and I'll make sure you get my next issue, it would be good to stay in touch anyway."

Now maybe you don't send out a newsletter, maybe you would offer to send relevant market data from time to time; in any case, I think you get the point, get the prospect's information. "Feed the hole."

Certainly, there are additional methods of prospecting, methods that every agent should ultimately be engaged in; contacting expireds in your market area, approaching FSBO's, seeking referrals from your S.O.I. These are essential prospecting methods; however the ABC's of Prospecting System looks to focus agents on the most basic of the prospecting methodologies. The prospecting activities I want you to focus on are those that can be executed effectively regardless of your experience, developed talent, or salesmanship.

I'm going to now direct your attention to the Prospecting Model on page 28. This is the Prospecting Model at the core of the ABCs of Prospecting system. What I'm going show you first is precisely where and how the majority of real estate sales professionals have historically dropped the ball with regard to prospecting. It is very interesting; and as you watch the magnitude of the blunder unfold, be honest, and ask yourself if you're guilty of the same.

Look first at the Prospecting Model as a flow chart. Follow the flow, if you will, of new prospects inbound to the database as well as the associated actions. These associated actions are the activities of CRM, Client Relationship Management.

Your objective in conducting diligent CRM is to establish and maintain rapport with your contacts. CRM is the process by which you convert contacts to prospects and subsequently, prospects to leads, and leads to closed transactions. This conversion process is the heart of the ABC's of Prospecting System. The Prospecting Model or flow chart details the conversion process.

It is important to understand that the hinge pin of the conversion process is the prospect meeting. Your objective must be to schedule and attend face to face meetings with prospects.

We'll pick up this discussion in a moment; I want to begin as promised with the age old error exhibited by the overwhelming majority of real estate sales professionals. As I detail the tremendous mistake, to ensure that you are able to follow closely don't refrain from referring as necessary to the Prospecting Model diagram.

Let's frame this illustration of events within a one week time frame, and let us further presume to begin with ten fresh contacts/prospects. Of course I have to preface this by asking that at least for the moment you imagine the large oval is not there.

O.k., the stage is set. A typical agent, (Agent Davis), with no true database begins a week with 10 new prospects. His objective is to communicate with each of them and try to schedule a meeting with each. Right away Agent Davis is able to determine that 2 of his contacts are not yet serious prospects, he now has 8 to work with. Agent Davis proceeds to call the remaining prospects. Resulting from this direct communication, Agent Davis further discovers that 2 more of the individuals are not quite at that level of readiness; one of them had some credit issues she was diligently working to resolve and the other, awaiting a determining series of events at his place of employment, (something about a pending transfer). An additional 2, simply were not able to set appointments this week. Agent Davis is still feeling good about the meetings he was able to schedule with the remaining 4 prospects.

The meetings prove to be quite revealing. Agent Davis discovers that of the 4 prospects, he can reasonably assess that 2 of them are "ready to go" right now. Of the 2 not "ready to go", 1 was about 60 days out and the other wanted to give the market a little more time to develop in his favor. Not a problem for Agent Davis, he's fully prepared to move forward with the 2 "clients in-hand". As events progress Agent Davis unfortunately realizes that 1 of his clients, due to personal developments, must post-pone for at least 90 days. No worry for Agent Davis, he's in contract a few weeks later with his 1 remaining client of the original 10 contacts. Shortly thereafter, Agent Davis will close escrow and look to move on to begin a new week with 10 fresh contacts.

Where did our Agent Davis drop the ball? Are you guilty of the same oversight? You may be thinking, "drop the ball, Davis had a great week! He successfully worked 10 contacts resulting in a closed transaction!" Well yes he did, but let's take a closer look.

Where Agent Davis dropped the ball, was his failure to understand the value of opportunity. What about the OTHER NINE PROSPECTS? With no database, Agent Davis had no place to "bank" the other nine prospects, nor did he have any real reason, in his mind, to consider them at all.

This is representative of the age old error of a staggering number of real estate sales professionals. Yes he closed a deal, but shortly after his escrow closed, Agent Michaels of a competing brokerage closed escrow with one of Agent Davis' original 10. Why? Because her credit issues were not as critical as was first thought and having no real ties or loyalty to Agent Davis, when ready, she responded to an advertisement of Agent Michaels who was all to pleased to assist her. Shortly afterwards, Agent Jones, from Agent Davis' own office was closing escrow with yet another of Davis' original 10 because his job transfer went forward and he needed to list his home after all. He actually liked Agent

26

Davis, but that was weeks ago and he could not remember Davis' name, just the office he worked in. Having called the office, but not having a clue as to Davis' name he had no objection to being put through to an available agent; after all, he had to sell his home quickly now.

Need I go on? It is a tremendous waste and represents a major lost opportunity, or multiple ones to have simply allowed those other nine prospects to fall to the way side. To make matters worse, five years after Agent Davis closed that escrow, the past client, whom he never databased nor contacted again, sold that home and purchased a larger one with Agent Bryant of another brokerage because although they were satisfied with Agent Davis' service, they could not begin to recollect his name or even which office he worked out of.

What the ABC's of Prospecting System provides you with is the skill set, tools, and ability to database those contacts, maintain communication with them, as well as build rapport through a process of incubation so that when they do reach that state of readiness, YOU will be the agent of choice. In short, you will know how not to foolishly follow in the footsteps of Agent Davis and so many others.

Let's discuss what you should be doing, diligent, effective warm contact management; CRM.

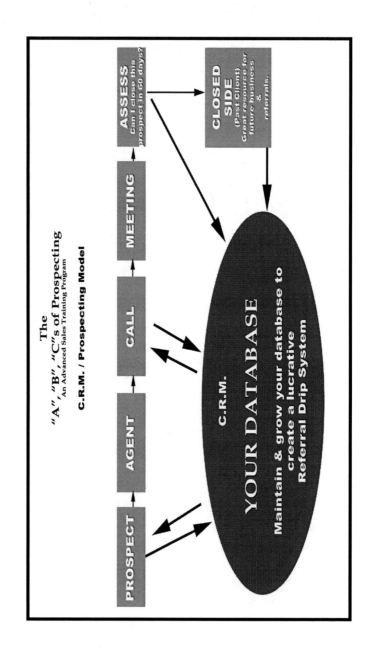

The
"A", "B", "C"s of Prospecting
An Advanced Sales Training Program

C.R.M. / Prospecting Model

PROSPECT — AGENT — CALL — MEETING — ASSESS
Can I close this prospect in 60 days?

CLOSED SIDE
(Past Client)
Great resource for future business & referrals.

C.R.M.
YOUR DATABASE
Maintain & grow your database to create a lucrative Referral Drip System

28

Take a look again if you will at the Prospecting Model diagram on the previous page. Hopefully the experience of our Agent Davis helped you to realize the importance of that oval.

Where do you have your contacts databased? Some agents use their PDA, others use Outlook, and there are those who simply use a spreadsheet file format perhaps in MS Excel. If you are one such agent, I applaud you for having your contacts databased. However, my suggestion to you is that you very seriously look into obtaining a CRM software platform. I assure you that such an investment will return enormous dividends at the end of the day.

A worthwhile CRM tool will include database management, leads management, and ideally a module for automated or automatic marketing via email; eFarming. A few such available tools include SalesAspects, by NetAspects, or Inteli-Contact, V-Lender, Top Producer 7i, etc.

The true purpose here is to ensure that no contact is ever wasted. Further, to ensure that your conversion processes continue. Your ability to handle 250 contacts or more and to execute diligent CRM must be questioned if you are not leveraging your ability to do so by employing the aide of technology. In short, CRM technology tools will ensure that your CRM plan is evenly and equally applied across the board, to each of your contacts.

The reason most agents fail to perform with regard to CRM is the reason many agents are not properly working a geographical farm; the required consistency simply proves to be too much. Successful execution of a CRM action plan, much like a farming action plan requires absolute consistency. Most agents simply do not possess the discipline or the patience to sustain the necessary persistence and follow through. Using leverage to overcome such shortcomings is what the ABC's of Prospecting System can offer. Technology certainly is one means of leverage but even more powerful in this regard is the application of systems, operational systems, systems such as the ABC's of Prospecting.

Operational systems can remove a great deal of the burden of consistency from the agent. The ABC's of Prospecting provides such relief in the form of an action plan. Following the plan should be systematically approached.

A little bit later in this book I will cover this systematic approach and detail the action plan. For now, let's briefly revisit the Prospecting Model. We've already addressed the fact that to do your true job as a real estate sales professional you must prospect. Whereas you must be a presence in your market area and seek the information of, and database everyday persons with whom you cross paths.

What must follow is the practice or execution of sound CRM activities in order to establish and maintain rapport with these contacts. You must endeavor to orchestrate your conversion processes. The Prospecting Model details the flow of these primary conversion processes.

Your objective in communicating with your prospects is to obtain that face to face meeting. During that meeting you will need to assess the prospect's state of readiness. Ask yourself; "Can I initiate a buy, sell, or finance transaction involving this individual within the next sixty days?" Whereas, given your assessment of each prospect's readiness you must determine whether or not it is plausible to be in contract, (open escrow), in service of this person within sixty days. If so, proceed as such; if not, plan to continue the cultivation and incubation of those individuals.

Take a look back at our Prospecting Model again. The rectangles indicate the sequence of events associated with the activities of the model involving the direct communication with prospects. The oval, as I have referred to it now several times, represents the database and the functions relative to database management and CRM.

Please take note of the larger of the arrows indicating flow to and from the database. Recall now the actions in error of our Agent Davis. In the sequence of events of direct communications with his prospects, Agent Davis dropped at first 2 contacts, then 4 more, followed by another 2, and then finally 1 more. Each of those prospects dropped and essentially forgotten by Agent Davis would be returned directly to the database for further incubation until the state of readiness reached a point of action. Once ready with any issues of delay eliminated or overcome, the arrows indicate their return to the actionable sequence of communication.

I like to think of the database as a wheel, or perhaps a barrel churning slowly, powered by CRM, cultivating contacts for future business. Lastly, let us not forget Agent Davis' client whom he represented to a fully closed transaction. This individual is now a past client and should absolutely be placed back into the "barrel". Past clients are presumably satisfied with your services and are an excellent source of future business and immediate, as well as long term referrals; ONLY if you continue your conduct of CRM even upon them.

As I stated previously, CRM done right, requires the right plan. The right plan of action for prospecting and conducting successful CRM upon your database will most certainly lay the ground work for consistency. Recall, that consistency, or the lack thereof, is where most sales agents fail.

Having a viable database alone is not the means to success. It is but a component of such success. What are you doing with your database? How is it organized, compartmentalized, and structured? Primarily, what activities are you engaged in to obtain, and maintain awareness in the minds of your contacts? In short, you have a database but do you have a solid plan to consistently work that database? Unfortunately, most agents will answer these questions with; "nothing really …actually its not ….none really ….. uh no, I guess I don't".

Let's begin with the structure of your database. In the following Lesson I detail this subject explicitly so as not to be redundant, I will not do so here. What should be mentioned is that it is absolutely necessary for the sake of efficiency, to apply a method of categorization to your database. CRM is essentially messaging or marketing specifically to select groups within your database. The key, besides consistency of communication, is that the communication, or messaging, be tailored toward the individuals receiving it. All this means is you don't want to send a message geared toward first time buyers to investors, or prospective sellers in your database. You also would not want to communicate to prospects that are perhaps 6 to 8 months out, with the same frequency you communicate to those who are 30 days out. Different strokes for different folks, your database structure must reflect this.

I suppose it makes sense when detailing a plan of action, to discuss the actions. The graphic on page 36 is the Prospecting Action Plan of the ABC's of Prospecting System. The left column vertically displays the contact categories of the system, A through D. The adjacent column provides a description of the contact category. Under the "Actions" heading, you will note definitive recommended actions to be taken with regard to each prospect category; the frequency of the action is also detailed.

The actions of the ABC's of Prospecting System include the following:

- **eFarming – targeted messaging via email**
- **Telephone Contact – the 2 minute phone call**
- **Visitation – getting face to face with your prospects**
- **Snail Mail – yet another link in the chain of consistency**
- **Individual/Personal emailing – direct email communications**

Remember, the name of the game is consistency! If you were consistently utilizing only one method or just a single tool for contact, your prospects would likely begin to regret ever having spoken with you. Variety is a good thing; it keeps the prospects interested and ensures that you yourself don't become bored or discouraged with the process.

The
"A", "B", "C"s of Prospecting
An Advanced Sales Training Program

Prospecting ACTION Plan

Category	Contact Description			ACTIONS		
"A"	*Likely to transact w/you* Warmest contacts GOOD Rapport ------- State of readiness determined to be w/in 30 days.	1 per month CRM eFarming Campaign Message "Prospect Relations" "Just Listed/Sold" message	1 per month CRM Telephone Call The "2 Minute Phone Call"	1 per Quarter Visitation Bring an item of interest/value	Snail Mail "Just Listed/Sold" Postcard, Flyer, Announcement, etc.	*Optional* Individual custom & personal email message
"B"	*Just met; new prospects* Moderate temperature GOOD Potential ------- State of readiness determined to be w/in 30 to 90 days.	1 per month CRM eFarming Campaign Message "Prospect Relations" "Just Listed/Sold" message	1 per WEEK CRM Telephone Call The "2 Minute Phone Call"	1 attempt per MONTH Visitation Bring an item of interest/value	Snail Mail "Just Listed/Sold" Postcard, Flyer, Announcement, etc.	*Optional* Individual custom & personal email message
"C"	*Possibly abrasive* Non-responsive COLD ------- State of readiness determined to be beyond 90 days.	1 per month CRM eFarming Campaign Message "Prospect Relations"				
"D"	DELETE					

Let's take a closer look at each of these activities. Much like the ABC's of Prospecting System itself, made up of several components integrated to produce the total power of the system; the actions of the Prospecting Action Plan are important individually, yet powerful when enacted together.

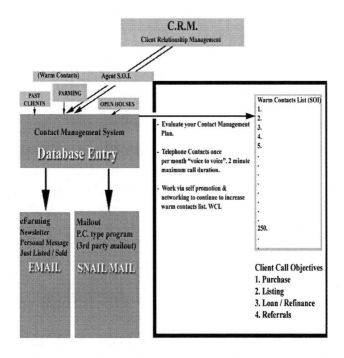

The graphic above is a flow chart demonstrating the flow of viable contacts from various sources into your database. Further, it displays the actions of the

Prospecting Action Plan and how they coalesce to provide the full impact of the system.

eFarming

eFarming is messaging electronically via email. I don't think I need to detail the importance of including methods within your plan to reach people online. With well over 70% of would be prospects in some fashion employing the internet in their real estate and finance process, it is imperative that you be present there as well and conduct activities designed to reach them there.

Sometimes eFarming content consists of market data, or perhaps a personal message. More frequently you want to use it simply to convey your competence as a sales professional.

Begin a consistent pattern of sending information to your database via email; perhaps a newsletter or market report. Learn the relatively simple process of incorporating images into your outgoing emails and distribute "*Just Listed*" and "*Just Sold*" announcements. Even if you don't have a current listing at the time of your mail out, use an office listing; just be certain not to take credit for the listing overtly as this could cause tension in the office. Generally speaking I never had an agent object to having notice of their listings disbursed to an additional database of prospective buyers.

You do not, of course, want to SPAM your contacts or inundate them with email. You do want to be a consistent presence in their inbox, yet you want that presence to be generally well received; you want to be sending messages of value as well as competence. Your newsletter, or market report, even an appropriately timed seasonal recipe would suffice; something of interest to them.

Snail Mail

The good old US Mail system, mix it up a bit. Periodically you're going to want to send actual items of value, and items of competence to your prospects via US Mail. Pretty hard to send those calendars and refrigerator magnets, pens and postcards via email. Each individual action in the Prospecting Action Plan is supplemental, and in support of the others.

P.C., or Preferred Client programs are widely available to agents today. Some brokerages run them in-house, and plenty of third-party providers have them for a fee as well. These programs automate the process of mail out. Often times they require very little, if any continued involvement form the agent. Provide them your database and for a fee, (includes postage- bulk rate), they will systematically distribute a predetermined sequence of items to your contacts. In many cases these items are highly customizable. The items vary, including postcards, seasonal greeting cards, letters, calendars, newsletters, etc. In any case, they are almost always branded; whereas your image, contact information and logo or brand is typically imprinted on each item. Generally, your prospects understand these items to be coming directly from you. Typically as you grow your contact database it is relatively easy to resubmit your database so it is always up-to-date.

Snail mail as it's called also serves to include those persons in your database who do not have an email address; or more commonly those for whom you have not yet obtained one.

Telephone Contact

Arguably the most powerful component of the Action Plan is direct communication, the telephone call; second only to visitation. In coaching sessions with sales agents I have the most fun demonstrating this component; the dubious, 2 minute phone call. I instruct agents to get into the habit of calling each person on there contact list once per month. The purpose of the call is quite simply just to stay in touch. To say essentially, you're in my thoughts, just wanted to reach out and say hello, or simply to say "hey, how are you?"

This is NOT a sales call! It is very important to understand that you are not making these calls to "hard sell" anyone. In fact, I instruct agents to not even bring up the subject of real estate and to not allow the conversation to exceed 2 minutes. Wow! Here's where the fun begins.

"Wait, so you don't want me to discuss real estate?" "Two minutes; that's 120 seconds, that's impossible!"

As you can imagine these are common responses; you're quite possibly muttering the same right at this moment. I assure you it is possible, and under the pressure of a second hand on a doubting agent's watch, I have NEVER failed to prove it.

Now before you leap to the conclusion that I must have lost it today somewhere between breakfast and Lesson 4, let me explain the process and the reasoning. The purpose of the call is to retain, or maintain rapport, it is a friendly hello. If you're following the plan then your contacts are already receiving plenty of real estate and finance related material from you. In this age where you would be hard pressed to find someone without Caller I.D., you want to actually get through to the people you are calling. If your call has become something they dread, or would simply rather not deal with, where does that leave you and are you really building rapport?

Keep it light; discuss what's going on with them. Ask how the kids are, or how that weekend getaway worked out. Impress them with the fact that you truly just called to keep in touch.

Right now you're likely thinking; "with 250 contacts how am I supposed to remember who has kids or who was planning a weekend in Vegas?" Good question; the answer, you take notes. One of the Appendixes I have provided for you at the back of this book is the ABC's of Prospecting System Call Log. This is where you will keep brief notes each month about small details of your conversations with prospects. It does not require total recall. Believe me, your prospects will be genuinely impressed and often a bit moved by the fact that you remembered a few tiny details from your last conversation.

Hopefully you're starting to understand this process a bit now although I imagine there's still a little doubt in your mind regarding the 2 minute limitation. Below, I have scripted what very plainly mirrors the typical flow of one of these telephone calls. Time it if you wish, you may be genuinely surprised at how little time an actual full conversation can require.

Agent: *Hey Tom, Agent Davis here, how are you?*

Prospect: *Oh, hi Davis. I'm fine. What can I do for you?*

Agent: *Oh nothing Tom, I just wanted to give you a call, just keeping in touch. Hey did Tom Jr. get into his first choice school?*

Prospect: *Oh yeah, hey thanks for asking. He sure did, and 2 others as well.*

Agent: *Tom that's great! I know you and Debra must be overflowing with pride!*

Prospect: *Yeah, we sure are. 17 years in the making. Now all we have to do is pay for it right. You know we've got funds set aside but you know, it's just never enough.*

Agent: *Tom, believe me I know what you're talking about. Hey, have you looked into scholarship programs, financial aide? They can really be a big help.*

Prospect: *Oh sure we have, believe it or not we make too much money to qualify for most of them.*

Agent: *It's like a double edged sword, I know.*

Prospect: *Yeah, you can say that again. Davis, I know you're in real estate but do you handle finance as well? Debra and I talked about our equity position and thought maybe we could re-fi or something.*

Agent: *Tom, I do and I would be happy to help out. The lending environment is so permissive right now and there are so many loan and finance options available. Tell you what; I've got some time this evening; how about I stop by and lay out some of your options more clearly? And hey, tell Tom Jr. I have a software program I can bring him. He can load it on his lap top and have it at school; it's an organizational tool for college kids, helps them stay organized at school you know?*

Prospect: *Wow Davis that would be absolutely fantastic. Are you sure it's not too much trouble?*

Agent: *Of course not Tom. How about between 6:30 and 7:00?*

Prospect: Absolutely*! I'll let Debra know, I think she's making pasta....or something.*

Agent: *See ya then Tom.*

Did you time that exchange? What you've just read through is very similar to an actual experience not to long ago. By relating this conversation to you, it is my hope that you can see it is certainly possible to have a full, rich conversation within 2 minutes. One of the reasons it's important to keep the call to 2 minutes is because you've got many more to make! You must consider the potential opportunity cost if you stay on the call with one prospect simply chatting for a half an hour and as result are prohibited from continuing down your list. Perhaps you make only 11 calls instead of 32. In the scenario scripted above, you should not take the opportunity to get into the options discussion with Tom on the phone, foregoing the remaining persons on your list for the day. Rather, use the opportunity to gain the face to face meeting, get off the phone with Tom and continue your calls.

I know what you're thinking, "didn't you say NOT to discuss real estate or finance?" No I didn't...... I said I instruct agents to not *bring up the subject* of real estate or finance; in other words, do not initiate such dialogue. What you may have discovered in your time as a real estate sales professional is that many people want to speak to you, even more so, many people enjoy personally knowing a knowledgeable real estate professional. They are pleased to let friends and associates know of their relationship with you. It is empowering to be able to speak knowledgeably regarding real estate and finance. Invariably you will find that the prospect will be the one to initiate such dialogue, usually to get your opinion or comment on something they may have heard regarding the market.

The question or comment is your open door, now you may step right through it, welcomed, invited, and accepted. If no such opportunity presents itself, that's fine, finish the conversation pleasantly, let them know it's been great speaking with them and you'll look forward to doing so again in a few weeks. Enter any noteworthy comments or detail into the Call Log and proceed with the next call.

This is a business, yes; but it is one built of personal relationships, trust, rapport, and often mutual respect, where the ones who reach true benchmark levels of success, are personable, and sociable with an understanding of how to relate those attributes to a professional standard of practice.

Your conduct of good CRM requires that you have the ability to be a good relationship manager. Establishing the relationships and maintaining them is important of course, but you must learn to manage them to serve your real estate sales business. Much like a good personnel manager is able to increase departmental productivity or efficiency by skillfully managing the personnel subordinate to her; you as a real estate professional must skillfully manage your database and the relations with the prospects who are so clearly vital to your productivity and overall success. It's simply CRM done right.

LESSON FIVE – The Real A's, B's, and C's

The real "A", "B", "C's"; prospect categorization based upon established rapport and state of readiness, (how soon are they projected to act).

As you can no doubt see from the Prospecting Model previously discussed, at the heart of the ABCs of Prospecting system is your database. If your database is the heart of the system, then database management is the pulse of that heart.

By now you should possess an understanding of what database management is; what it means to manage your database.

Database management is a great deal like course management in golf. An example of course management would be knowing that when facing a lengthy par 4 that dog legs about 190 yards from the tee, you may want to keep the driver in the bag and angle a long iron along the far side. In other terms, database management is all about how you appropriately use the tools at your disposal based on the circumstances and environment to exact the best result.

What I'm saying I've said a few times already, it's not enough to simply have a database, you need to use it. More importantly, you need to use it effectively.

The ABCs of Prospecting system is aptly named for the system of database categorization it advocates:

- **"A" level prospects**
- **"B" level prospects**
- **"C" level prospects**

There is of course another prospect category, "D", but we'll get to that in a bit. The purpose of such categorization is to compartmentalize. The reason is specificity, or targeted marketing.

The objective of conducting effective CRM can only be achieved if your messaging is appropriately distributed. It can be as obvious as not sending a sellers' oriented message out to first time buyers or as subtle as the frequency with which you send messages. There are several benefits to categorization of your database, including:

- **Being able to identify your volume of potential business**
- **Knowing your prospect ratios – buyers to sellers, or loan prospects**
- **Having the ability to engage in targeted marketing**
- **Evaluating your pipeline value and timelines**
- **The ability to review specific response data, to evaluate marketing efforts**

Not to mention for the sheer benefit of sanity. Can you imagine attempting to manage a database of 200 to 400 contacts with no such categorization, no structure? Can you say……. migraine?

The ABC's of Prospecting system provides you the structure, and the organizational model for your contacts database. Naturally I recommend the categorization of your database by the grouping of whom, and what each contact is or represents. I call these "marketing groups". Some of the marketing groups I advise agents to use are:

- **Buyers**
- **Sellers**
- **1st Time Buyers**
- **Finance**
- **Investors**
- **Peers (other agents)**

- **S.O.I. (sphere of influence)**
- **Past Clients**
- **Farm Residents (persons living within your geographical farm area)**
- **Everyone (all of your contacts)**

These are merely suggestions, it really is subjective, whereas you want to personalize your database, and the structure must work for you.

Database marketing groups are essential to distributing appropriately scripted messages, yet they are not at the core of the ABC's of Prospecting system. Marketing groups more succinctly determine the message for your marketing campaigns. They are representative of the "who's" and the "what's" of your database. Is this person a buyer, are they a past client, is she your sister-in-law?

Important to note, contacts can belong to multiple marketing groups. Allen Smith can be a member of your S.O.I., and be a bona fide refinance prospect as well. Anne Durant can be both a past client and an investor.

Absolutely, marketing groups are an essential part of your database structure and I highly recommend you utilize them. However, the ABC's of Prospecting is much more than a marketing system; it is a CRM system at its core and therefore is more kindred to timelines, prospect relationship "temperature", and readiness.

"A", "B", and "C" are not marketing groups, they are database or contact categories. Contact categories are not a representation of whom, or what each prospect may be; but rather the indicators of the prospects state of readiness. They are the determining factor with regard to the degree of action, or CRM activity appropriate for each prospect.

Remember, this is all about conversion processes. Generally speaking, it is about converting cold contacts, to warm prospects. The ABC's of Prospecting system is your internal, conversion engine for organic leads generation.

When was the last time you were at the bakery and initiated a casual conversation with a person in line with you and as you identified yourself as a real estate agent, too your great surprise they said; "wow, I was hoping I ran into a real estate agent today! Would you come home with me, I'm ready to sell my house; be sure to bring your Listing Agreement! Get your truffles first, of course."

You know, I'm sure if I pole enough agents, eventually I'll find someone who says this or something similar has happened to them. I'll concede, I'm sure it happens, it's a crazy world and at times, a funny business we're in. However, understand that it is at best, rare. The overwhelming majority of the time gap between that chance encounter, and a closed transaction is going to require conversion; an elevation in the relationship temperature.

In Lesson Four you were introduced to the Prospecting Action Plan. If you take another look at it you will note that what you are in fact looking at is the process by which you elevate, steadily elevate, the temperature of your prospect relationships. Often it is not even restricted to the readiness of a prospect to personally need your services. You are building your rapport, you are establishing your competence, and their confidence in your professional ability. This transcends mere personal need, you are creating an environment of trust, one where your prospects will generate and deliver referrals to you.

I've heard it said that referrals are the Holy Grail of our business. I disagree; the statement would have my endorsement if it were; a prospect willing to frequently and consistently feed you referrals is the Holy Grail of our business. Now that, I'll buy into!

Let's take a closer look at each of the categories.

D

Delete! The mere mention of the word makes me cringe. If the idea here is to continually look to increase your total database, deleting individuals is, or should be a regretful act. Talk about counter-productive! As such, you certainly want to use it sparingly. I generally instruct agents to archive, rather than delete. Delete is so permanent and so negative. You can archive a contact or if you're using a capable CRM platform/software, you can usually opt them out; essentially they remain in your database but are blocked from receiving email messages from you.

This category is reserved for those contacts who have actually requested not to receive anything from you. These are individuals for whom there is virtually no hope. Once again, the ABC's of Prospecting system requires you to utilize your assessment skills. Generally if a contact is rude, dismissive, seemingly annoyed, or just consistently non-responsive, they rightfully belong in the "D" category. Remember always, this is a business, your business. You can ill afford to consume expense or human resource trying to manage contacts where you can assess the effort to be futile. Just be certain, as certain as you can be. It could be a terrible waste to discard even a remotely potential contact.

C

Cold, and are often non-responsive. "C" category prospects differ from the "D's" in that their non-responsiveness is typically directly associated with their state of readiness. Generally beyond 90 or 120 days, these are the prospects who say things like;

"Yeah, I appreciate the call Agent Laura, but I was just surfing your web site a bit just to kind of see what's out there. Jim and I probably won't be looking to actually make a move for another 6 months or so."

This contact may become non-responsive, not because they dislike you; but rather they simply are not ready to really start the process. Hey, she told you she was six months or more out; take her word for it. However, this is still a viable contact. As I'm sure our fictitious Agent Davis would likely attest, it would leave an awful taste in your mouth if she contacted the next agent in six months to list her $400k home and to assist in purchasing their new $600k home. So, you absolutely would want to keep this person in your active database and continue to execute your CRM model upon her. However, you want to back off a bit, give her the appropriate space yet still work to build the rapport that will, when the time is right, ensure that you are the agent of choice.

Another good example of a "C" category prospect would be someone who was initially a "B" category prospect but had perhaps a credit score situation arise. Perhaps it was your consultation that helped them realize the reality of their options. Instead of settling and buying beneath their needs and wants they decided to contract a credit repair service provider, recommended by you of course, and give it six months. Naturally this is a situation where you most certainly want to stay in touch.

Remember, although this is a conversion process which you want to keep slanted in one direction, it is also about "course management", temperature control; it can be sensitive at times and beyond your control. You're cultivating prospects here, much like flowers in a garden; some will require more or less management. As you apply this model, and the ABC's of Prospecting system, you will likely find the majority of movement of contacts between or back and forth from "B" to "C" as well as the reverse.

B

The "B" category is the proving ground; most of your new prospects will enter your database as "B" category contacts. From here they will either be converted to "A" or "C" category contacts. It will not be uncommon for prospects here to reach an immediate state of readiness; a direct conversion to transaction, (Client), status.

The "B" category is where you have the most frequent or intensive CRM efforts prescribed. The purpose for this is because it is here where you will truly be seeking to make determinations about each prospect. As you apply the ABC's of Prospecting system consistently, you will begin to realize that you are becoming quite skilled at assessing prospects accurately, and doing it in a much timelier manner.

Visitation is a large part of the CRM protocol for "B" category prospects. It is your objective to aggressively seek face to face meetings with these individuals. Doing so will sharply increase your ability to accurately assess their status.

Also, these prospects have a higher likelihood for activity in the short term. You certainly would not want them to respond to, or go the way of another agent should they become ready within short notice. Say for instance, if you were only communicating with them once per month; that leaves plenty of room for them to be lost to another agent. Let's be frank, just because you send something to a prospect doesn't mean they necessarily see it. Not all mailings are received or viewed, thus the need for frequency and redundancy. The "B" category is your bread and butter, never loose site of this, or of the prospects in it.

A

Welcome home! The "A" category is your safe place, your warm haven. Why? This category primarily consists of your warmest contacts, your S.O.I., friends, family members, co-workers if you're a part-time agent perhaps. These are people for whom a higher level of aggression or frequency with regard to CRM, is not necessary.

The necessary degree of contact may be sufficient at lower levels but it is absolutely necessary to include such warm contacts in your CRM efforts. Again, why?

Have you ever had a sales agent, "I don't believe it" moment? This often occurs at family gatherings when you're visiting, the house is full of your closet friends and family members. Invariably, a cousin, or in-law, or Aunt, or a friend gets a phone call on their cell. They step out momentarily to converse. Upon their return someone more aware than you notices a change in that person's expression, their energy level; the person is clearly excited. They say, "that must have been some phone call, to which the excited individual replies" it sure was, my real estate agent showed our home yesterday and the people submitted a strong offer today!"

At that moment, your heart sinks, and either you say it out loud, under your breath, or you simply say it to yourself; "I don't believe it! Hello! What about me? You know, your dear relative who happens to be a real estate agent!"

Sound at all familiar? If not, you're doing something right. Trust me when I tell you this scenario repeats itself the world over everyday. As agents, you get tied up, you get bogged down with some of the "busy work", I know. As a result, a thing like communicating ON A PROFESSIONAL LEVEL with relatives seems to somehow, not occur.

It's not that you don't see or speak to them; you simply do not do so often enough on a professional level. Given the opportunity, I'm sure the majority of persons in your family or your inner-most sphere of influence would absolutely refer prospects your way. However, the burden is not on them to remember your real estate career; it's on YOU to remind them.

It is not so much a matter of marketing, to your "A" category contacts, it is more a manner of non-aggressive, yet consistent CRM. It can be quite sobering to begin to think about GCI you could be loosing annually as your closet relations refer their S.O.I. to other agents.

Treat your "A" category as though it is your savings bank. Place contacts in this category with this thought; it's money in the bank! A diligent and steady CRM effort in their direction is a guarantee of future business, either direct or by referral. It is here among these individuals that you will look to build your referral base. Do it right and that base will serve you indefinitely; do it right and your "A" category prospects will become your army of advocates.

Much like your primary marketing campaign, or the physical necessary expenses of your real estate sales business, CRM has associated costs. As I have stated previously this is first and foremost, a business. As such, you should have an expectation of "return" for every dollar expended or invested in your business.

I'm speaking of course about R.O.I., or Return On Investment. Your CRM related expense will likely be moderate but you should still have an expectation of fiscal return. Ah, but how do you quantify such a return and what constitutes a reasonable expectation of return? Great questions I'm sure you will agree. Well, a quick rule of thumb is what I refer to as the "relative time" rule. Simply stated, this is a means to quantify expenditures and gauge your expectation of return, relative to the timeframe or duration of the activity.

Let's try this rule out on a hypothetical, but typical agent geographical farm. I recently utilized this rule to complete a CBA, (cost benefit analysis), of one years worth of farming activity. I did so for the purpose of demonstration for group of experienced agents I was coaching. The CBA is printed below.

Let's assume that your average net commission on a listing is $7,000. If you only get one additional listing a year from your direct mail campaign to your farm, you "profit" as long as you spend less than $7,000 in this effort in that year.

How realistic is this?

Well, let's figure you mail out to your farm two times every month and each direct mail piece cost a total of .67c. [.39c postage, .13c printing, .15c stuffing, labeling, & mailing]; that's $1.34 per piece and $2.68 per home, per month. Divide $7,000 by 2.68 and you get approximately 2,612. Divide 2,612 by 12 (months) – and you can mail to 218 homes, twice each month for the entire year with a $7,000 annual cost.

In other words, you "breakeven" if you get one listing from mailing to 218 homes twice each month.

If you get two listings, for example, your "breakeven" point moves up to 435 homes reached twice each month.

What's more, if you can cross promote, (and split costs), with a vendor or lender, you can further mitigate the total cost and increase your profit even more.

I use this as an example because I assume it is something you can relate to. The idea is that the justification of expense over a defined period of time is directly relative your production; whereas, you anticipate your return by manner of productivity. Decide how many transactions it is reasonable to expect as a result of your efforts. The fact is, your commission split and commission earned percentage can be established as fixed figures, and your average commission per transaction can be deduced using either your prior year data, or in the case of a farm, the average home value in the farm area.

The CBA model differs somewhat with regard to CRM, but the rule still applies. The relative time period with regard to CRM is determined by the life cycle of our industry product. In all sales fields, the product has a life cycle. In the case of real estate sales, that product is real estate, real property; the life cycle of that product is five years. That is to say that in general, people will sell a home, buy a home or move every five years.

The following diagram is a visual CBA detailing the cost benefit of applying the ABC's of Prospecting system over the five year cycle. It demonstrates the benefit resulting from the CRM expense related to a single prospect. One key assumption made is that your time has a value of $100 per hour.

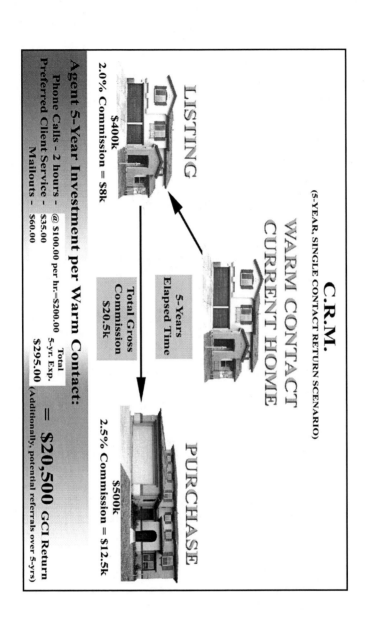

C.R.M.
(5-YEAR, SINGLE CONTACT RETURN SCENARIO)

WARM CONTACT CURRENT HOME

LISTING

$400k

2.0% Commission = $8k

5-Years Elapsed Time

Total Gross Commission $20.5k

PURCHASE

$500k

2.5% Commission = $12.5k

Agent 5-Year Investment per Warm Contact:

Phone Calls - 2 hours -	@ $100.00 per hr.=$200.00	Total
Preferred Client Service -	$35.00	5-yr. Exp.
Mailouts -	$60.00	$295.00

= **$20,500** GCI Return

(Additionally, potential referrals over 5-yrs)

65

Look closely at this graphic CBA; it also serves as a flow chart following the relationship or story over the five year term. Let me put words to this story, as a real estate agent, you should find this very interesting.

Let's say Agent Montano meets a new prospect at her favorite clothing boutique this week; we'll call this prospect Lisa, the boutique Owner. Getting to know Lisa, Agent Montano learns that her new prospect has one child and has been married to Todd for six years and that they just purchased their new home last month.

Clearly, Lisa and Todd are not at this time in need of Agent Montano's real estate sales services. However, being diligent Agent Montano places the couple in her contacts database initially as "C" category contacts. Over time, perhaps a year and some months, having seen Lisa several subsequent times at the boutique, Agent Montano has established a genuine rapport with Lisa and decides to place her and Todd in the "A" category of her database.

Let's jump ahead in time, about four more years. It's been just over five years since that original conversation in the boutique. Lisa and Todd are expecting their third child, Lisa is doing quite well at the boutique, and Todd has just landed a major promotion. They're looking for a larger home in an upscale neighborhood. Who do you think they're going to call? After five years' rapport established via consistent mailing of items of value and competence, telephone contact, email and face to face contact, Lisa and Todd are not likely to thumb through the phone book to find an agent. They absolutely call Agent Montano.

Agent Montano gladly lists their home. The pricing strategy she discussed with them results in a list price of $410k, a listing she takes for 2.0%. The home sells for $400k thus earning Agent Montano a gross commission of $8k. Don't forget about the other end, Agent Montano finds Lisa and Todd the home of their dreams; it's in their price range at $500k. Agent Montano earns a further gross commission in this transaction of 2.5%, or $12.5k bringing the total GCI to $20.5k.

Take a good look at the actual expense Agent Montano incurred establishing and maintaining the rapport with Lisa and Todd over the five year cycle. Start with the mail out expense. Lisa and Todd were "B", then "A" category prospects. As such they would have benefited from one snail mail, mail out per month. Over the five year span, that's 60 months x say $1 per month; $60. Additionally, when Agent Montano transitioned Lisa and Todd from the "B" to the "A" category, she enrolled or subscribed them in her Preferred Client Club service for an upfront cost of $35 for the full five year cycle.

Total expense incurred for mail out distribution over the five year period, $95.

Next we'll touch on something a little less tangible but easily and legitimately quantifiable; your time. First thing any entrepreneurial how-to guide or Guru is going to tell you is that you must place a dollar value on your time. I absolutely agree, establish it, and stick to it. I regularly instruct agents on this point and generally settle in somewhere around $100 per hr. You place what value on your time you determine appropriate.

Following the ABC's of Prospecting Action Plan, Agent Montano included one telephone call per month in her CRM protocol for the five year duration. At roughly 2 minutes per call, that's 120 minutes, or 2 hours x $100 per hour = $200.

Following this system, Agent Montano incurred a total expense in five years time of $295 relative to Lisa and Todd Siebel.

Wow! If that doesn't move you, you're in the wrong business. A $295 expense returns a gross income of $20.5k! That's better than most illegal industries I'll wager.

"But wait!"….. as the Aussie infomercial guy would say, "we're not finished yet!" As the sheer enormity of the exemplified R.O.I. sinks in, please consider this.

During the five year time period, given the established rapport, is it not conceivable that Lisa and Todd would have gladly been genuine advocates; a real source of referrals for Agent Montano? You better believe it! Hypothesize, how many times in five years did Agent Montano get an email from a referred new prospect? How many times did her phone ring because Lisa or Todd suggested to a friend, co-worker, or family member that they contact Agent Montano? How many such new inquiries resulted in a closed transaction; or a new "B" or "A" category prospect? Did Lisa and Todd refinance their home at any point during the time period?

Fortunately, I believe you are beginning to realize that the true benefit to your real estate sales career could be immeasurable.

I must attest that the numbers in our scenario above are real numbers; the return potential is genuinely that phenomenal. Sure, the numbers may vary based upon the home values in your market, or the income level of your average client. However; what will not vary, is the truly staggering potential R.O.I.

LESSON SEVEN – Advocates, Supporters, Believers and Followers

I recently attended a conference of Realtors® at which a new tool was introduced and being detailed to attendees. The product was Call Capture; next generation technology for our industry providing, among other things, leads capture by way of 24 hour property listing information. At this particular conference I was fortunate to hear a very special guest speaker. His name is Matthew Ferry and he is, to be short, a genius.

Matthew Ferry's specialty is what I would term, the psychology of sales. If you can accept that terminology, then accept also that Mr. Ferry has profound expertise in this regard. Much of what he teaches deals with an understanding of the power of language; the ability of words to exact a desired result; a desired response.

Ferry demonstrates to sales agents how to utilize this particular skill set, once developed, to build an army of sorts. It is no coincidence that the ABC's of Prospecting system ultimately affects the same result; an agent's army of advocates.

Ferry referred to the individuals comprising the army as the agent's advocates, supporters, believers, and followers. I agree.

As I listened to our guest speaker that day I could not help but to draw distinct parallels to the ABC's of Prospecting system. I thought of the manner of database categorization of the system, specifically of the "A" category. This category consists of those in your S.O.I., and your past clients; your CRM success stories as well. In an earlier Lesson I eluded to the extremely high value of the "A" category. If you haven't already, now you will begin to realize the power of advocates, supporters, believers, and followers.

Successful CRM is all about mindshare; branding yourself in the minds of prospects. Your "A" category individuals genuinely like you. They want to be advocates for you out in the world as they go about their lives. These persons want to support you, they believe in you; some of them, perhaps dear friends or family members from your S.O.I., would gladly follow your lead. How many people do you know like this? How many contacts have you cultivated to this level? How many referrals have those persons provided to you?

If you in fact do have such advocates, and you are doing your job correctly, they should be generating referrals. I would think that as an "end game" all agents should look to establish a referral based business. In order to do so you must conduct CRM upon even your closest relations. You must always look to keep satisfied, past clients in your inner-loop. Get family and friends involved, communicate with past clients. Make sure you have anniversary of closings campaigns ongoing. If the primary fruit of the "B" category are closed transactions, then the fruit of the "A" category most certainly, is the referral.

As an agent you want your army of advocates to be responsible for a significant volume of the sales leads you get. When this system is successfully applied, your advocates make your phone ring; again, and again, and again!

Now you may be thinking; how many brothers, sisters, parents, uncles and aunts, and best friends do you need to make this thing work?

That is sentiment indicative of a large, yet common misconception of many agents. Many agents tend to believe the S.O.I. refers only to close friends and family. This is simply untrue, and a grave error.

At the rear of this book as you will find the ABC's of Prospecting S.O.I. Mapping Tool. I want you to use this tool to expand forever your understanding and definition of your sphere of influence. Your S.O.I. is not exclusively comprised of your inner most circle. It should be inclusive of those individuals with whom you interact frequently. As you will no doubt notice when looking at the mapping tool, your S.O.I. includes, your butcher, baker, hair stylist, bank teller, tailor, postal delivery person, your child's coach, etc. Now, I'm sure it is safe to assume that you don't necessarily socialize with all of these people, or even most of them. What is common amongst them is the fact that you cross paths, or interact with them frequently; some of them even daily perhaps.

Think about that. There are people with whom you may have nearly daily contact; people you consider pleasant acquaintances, you may even refer to them by name. Consider the potential opportunities lost to you because you're neglecting CRM with regard to these warm contacts. Most agents and I do mean most agents, make the tremendously inappropriate assumption that because they've at some point in the past made reference to their real estate career to any of these persons, those persons will consider that fact, or even remember it when an opportunity is present.

You must conduct CRM even upon your warmest contacts; you must.

Remember the, "I don't believe it" moment from an earlier lesson? Picture this.

Your UPS guy Jens, comes to your door with your latest and greatest eBay acquisition.

Jens: *Hey Davis, how's it going today?*

Davis, (YOU): *Oh hey Jens, I'm good.*

Jens: *Another eBay buy eh? What is it this time?*

Davis: *This, my friend, is the coolest! It's a vintage "SOLD" sign, it gets bolted to my yard sign when I close; just a little touch of class.*

Jens: *Hey, maybe we could bolt it to the sign in front of my house. It's pending as of 2 weeks ago and people are still knocking on my door! Wait; you're in real estate?*

Now, I hate to ask the obvious but, how do you imagine you would feel at this point in the conversation? Even more so, how do you imagine you would feel after Jens told you he decided on an agent because that agent mailed a post card to his house?

People like our hypothetical Jens are not so hypothetical. You interact with them everyday, many of them. I wrote earlier of a shift in mindset. This is the manifestation of that shift. You must begin to open your eyes and see the abundance of prospects all around you. These individuals, these frequent encounters, most of them likely have no reason they would not be your advocate. No reasons other than you're failing to ask! Now, by "asking", I'm not referring to a direct assault; "hey, do you or anyone you know have any need for real estate services?" Not at all; I'm talking of course about CRM.

Consistent and diligent conduct of CRM, is to ask. You are letting them know that you are here, that you are a real estate sales professional. Effective CRM demonstrates that you are competent at what you do and that there is value in that. I constantly stress that CRM related mailings and distributions should include both items of value and items of competence.

This applies to even your closet relations. Your Aunt Dominique and Uncle Daylon may remember you as the ill-tempered, yet very cute "brat" they used to baby sit on occasion. It is important if they are to be your advocates, your supporters, that they realize little Marcelina has grown up and is a knowledgeable and competent real estate professional.

Your "A" category contacts are, or should be your most fervent believers. They are the ones who will continue to generate referrals for you and therefore they should always remain an essential part of your game plan.

Effective CRM cultivates, it incubates; this is why it is so very essential. It is the fuel of your conversion engine. CRM is how ordinary folks whose paths you cross can truly become the backbone of your business; advocates, supporters, believers, and followers.

Most of all I want users of the ABC's of Prospecting system to understand the purpose, benefit, and logic behind the system. Why is all of this necessary? What is the end game, so to speak?

Let's look at a few statistics.

Have you ever heard of the 87 / 13 rule? It stipulates that in any given year, only 13% of the revenue generated in our industry will come by way of direct advertisement; billboards, bus bench ads, news paper and magazine ad response, etc. It further stipulates that in that same year 87% of the revenue generated will be the direct result of warm contact management; CRM.

Think about that for a moment. That's not to say that direct advertisement is futile; not by any means.

After all, this sort of advertisement is what can provide you the raw contacts / prospects you need to put into your conversion engine. Such persons can be converted to "A" category contacts by way of your CRM model. I will never advocate the cessation of direct advertising efforts. What I am saying is to consider the rule as you allocate resources and time.

I'm certain you would agree that it makes very little sense to allocate a majority of your available resources such as your time, and budget chasing what is likely to produce only 13% of your revenue. Instead, would it not make a great deal more sense to allocate such resources to the pursuit of what will likely generate 87% of your revenue? The lesson here then would be to appropriately allocate resources towards warm contact management.

I spent time earlier discussing the value of building a referral based business. The ABC's of Prospecting system enables you in this regard. What you are creating is a referral drip system.

The following graphic illustrates the flow of such a system, the role that each element of the CRM model plays and, I believe, the tremendous value of warm contact management. This is all illustrated by picturing the database as the lemon within the vice. Further, it shows the steady, exertion of force upon

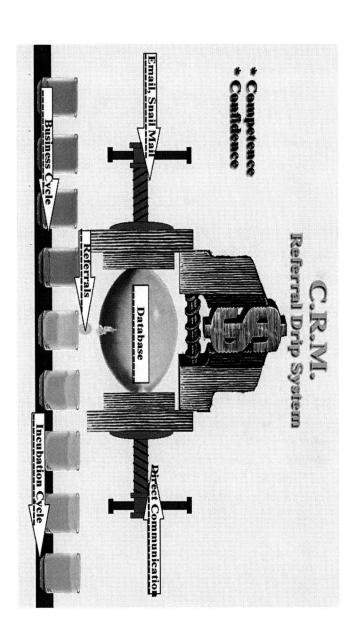

81

the database from the components of our CRM model, represented by the vice grips.

Interesting to note, the "squeeze" resulting from the "Direct Communication" component is appropriately illustrated as being equal to that of the combined email and snail mail components. This is meant to evidence the substantial influence of the 2 minute phone call; it cannot be overstated.

It is a relatively simple illustration. The applied forces of the CRM model components work in concert upon the raw prospects within the database. This is the heart of the conversion engine as contacts become warm contacts and subsequently the referral generating gems of your "A" contacts category.

The referral drip system is not an over night achievement; it takes time. CRM is more related to branding efforts; the efforts to achieve mindshare, it does take time. The conveyor belt at the bottom is meant to represent the cycle of the system. It must be ongoing; contacts never leave the database, ALL are recycled.

LESSON NINE – Good Luck, Good Fortune, and Happy Prospecting!

As a real estate sales professional you are in control of your own destiny. Truly; isn't that one of the reasons you opted to take this career path? Don't you enjoy the freedom of self employment?

With freedom comes great responsibility. Whereas, it is your business, ultimately the buck stops with you. Those steps necessary for your success are for you to take. Prospecting and CRM are components of success which require discipline. Many agents know precisely what they must do in order to succeed; they simply do not do it. They see other colleagues, top producers in their office perhaps, they know what these top producing agents are doing but lack the discipline to follow suit.

This business is not easy, though it is simple. This may sound like a contradiction in terms but it's not. You know what to do, the path to success is quite frankly, fairly plain to see. Knowing the path and walking the path are two different animals. Where most agents fail is in the execution. Knowing the plan is simple; the difficulty commonly comes in the execution of the plan.

Execution requires action, consistent, repetitive action as well as follow through. Unfortunately, for many agents, it becomes somewhat like a New Year's resolution diet. You attack it with earnest and good intention, you may even drop a couple of pounds but eventually, it becomes too much of a task and the plan is abandoned. Well don't blame the diet; you're the one who stopped, you were eating Big Mac's three weeks into January!

The ABC's of Prospecting system is your prospecting and CRM plan. You have been shown a very precise path to ultimate success as a real estate sales professional. You must now execute the plan and walk the path. Your current level of productivity will be enhanced; regardless of what that level is, if you wish to elevate your performance, this system can facilitate your ascent to that next level.

Apply your resources wisely. You should be spending 80% of your time towards warm contact management. I don't care if you're part time, or full time. Time is one of your most valued resources, as you consider your time management model, factor 80% of the time allocated to your career on warm contact management efforts and activities. Use the tools of the ABC's of Prospecting system to conduct such activities. Apply the models everyday, recall and frequently refer to the lessons conveyed in this book.

Work to build your database daily and be mindful of the strategies of communication for each of your prospect categories. Take good care of your "A" category contacts and they shall return the favor.

Much of our profession was built on trial and error. Many agents have come before you. Through their successes and failures we have the very fortunate opportunity to learn, and apply models that work. With such precedence available to you, it is foolish to look to reinvent the wheel. Stop making the mistakes of the past. The truest path to your ultimate success is very clear. CRM is not a recent development, it has been the key to the development of successful sales businesses for many, many years yet it is a relatively unpracticed model.

Similarly, I think it's safe to say that most agents realize the benefit of a referral based business, yet many do nothing to create an environment where one will develop. One of the most common errors amongst our ranks is one concerning referrals.

Agents for the most part are aware of the need to reward, or provide incentive for those advocates and supporters when they generate referral business for you. I advise agents to reward the act, not the result. Think about it; have you ever rewarded an individual for providing a referral or a lead to you? At what point did you give them the reward, at what point did you ultimately show your gratitude?

Many agents make the mistake of rewarding the result. They express their gratitude if, and only if the referral leads to a closed transaction. Reward the act; you should be very grateful when a contact generates a lead for you. You should express that gratitude in the form of a reward immediately after the referral comes in. Regardless of the eventual outcome, your job is to grow your database; an inbound lead by way of referral is certainly a step in that direction. Develop your army of advocates; make sure they understand the value you place on new contacts.

It has been my great pleasure to introduce you to the ABC's of Prospecting system. A great deal went into the initial creation of the system and the ensuing evolution has resulted in what is certainly the most specific CRM model you can apply to your real estate sales career. The fact is that the system can be applied by sales professionals of all industries. This is how the business of sales is done.

I feel confident that you have gained a particular understanding of your sales business from a different perspective; the only perspective that matters. That is the perspective of high achievement.

My personal wish is for your ultimate success and prosperity. It is my hope that you will employ the ABC's of Prospecting system to accomplish your productivity goals and elevate your career to the highest level of achievement.

In closing I bid you good luck, good fortune, and happy prospecting!

OHT – Objection Handling Technique

TELEPHONE SCRIPT
For INITIAL LEAD CAPTURE
COMMUNICATION

This script is to be applied for initial communication with all **live inbound telephone** prospects.

Thank you for contacting _____.
May I have your name please? How may I assist
you Mr./Ms. _____?

Wonderful, I can certainly assist you with that.
May I ask how you heard about or decided to
contact me today?

Excellent! Mr./Ms. _____ , my task, I feel is
to create the best possible environment to serve
your real estate and finance needs. This requires
only a few answers to some basic questions. May I
have your email address?

Are you currently working with a real estate agent?
(IF YES) That's fine; can I get your agent's name
and company name? As a courtesy I will contact

him/her to provide other properties in the area you may have an interest in.

*What would you say your likely time-frame to PURCHASE/SELL your home is? [(This qualifies the prospect as "A", "B", or "C".) IF longer than 30 days, please refer to bottom of page. IF <u>within</u> 30 days, it is an "A" prospect, please proceed.......]
That's fine. (IF BUYER) *I have great relationships with several loan specialists to assist with any finance concerns you may have; may I ask if you have been pre-qualified by a lender yet?*

O.K. (If BUYER calling about specific property) *I would like very much to schedule a showing appointment for you so you can get a first hand look at the property you've called in about. What is the next available convenient time and day for you; would you be available tomorrow?*

(IF BUYER OF A GENERAL INQUIRY) *Mr./Ms.*
_____, *the best way to research and view multiple properties of a similar nature is with the assistance of a professional Realtor®. I would like very much to schedule a first hand showing appointment for you so you can get a thorough look at the properties currently in the market that you would likely be interested in. What is the next available convenient time and day for you; would you be available tomorrow?*

(FOR SELLERS) *You know Mr./Ms. _____, the absolute best way for any Realtor® to professionally assess your home's value, market potential and appeal is to see it first hand. I would like very much to schedule a no obligation marketing consultation appointment with you. This first hand look will enable me to answer any questions you may have as well as begin to assess the full market potential of your home. What is the next available convenient time and day for you; would you be available tomorrow?*

That's wonderful Mr./Ms. _____, I have enjoyed speaking with you. Thank you for contacting me. I look forward to serving you further!

"B" and "C" Prospects:

That's fine, and perfectly understandable. We know this is typically a very big decision. It is one that really shouldn't be considered without the assistance of a professional Realtor®. I would like very much to schedule a no obligation consultation appointment with you. It's helpful to be able to benefit from professional experience early in the process. What is the next available convenient time and day for you; would you be available tomorrow?

(IF NO TO THE MEETING) *That's fine. I understand you simply may not be ready yet.*

Mr./Ms. _____, *my objective, always is to provide the highest quality client service possible. To that end, I would be pleased to stay in touch with you to serve you as you move closer towards your decision and to provide assistance in making that decision.*

I have enjoyed speaking with you. Please remember, always, my consultations are no obligation! Thank you for contacting me. I look forward to serving you further!

TELEPHONE SCRIPT
For <u>INITIAL</u> LEAD CAPTURE
COMMUNICATION
(*OUTBOUND CALL*)

This script is to be applied for **initial** communication for all **outbound calls placed** to "BUYER" prospects resulting from inbound <u>electronic leads</u> or return phone calls.

Hello Mr./Ms._____, My name is_____, I'm a Realtor® with _____. How are you doing today?

Wonderful! I'm calling in response to your recent on-line property search or inquiry. This is a courtesy follow-up call just to ensure all your real estate needs are currently being met.

First of all I would like to thank you for choosing my website, did you find the online and automated resources useful?

Very good! I have even more information and services that you may not have access to. I can even get you pre-qualified; have you talked to a lender about loan pre-qualification yet?

I would like very much to schedule a no obligation consultation appointment with you to ensure your needs get met. What is the next available convenient time and day for you; would you be available tomorrow?

Excellent, I will look forward to seeing you then.

(IF NO TO AN APPOINTMENT)
That's fine. What I will do in the mean time is register you for our exclusive e-mail notification. When properties become available on MLS that match your search preferences you will be among the first to preview them, and please don't hesitate to call if you see a listing that catches your interest.

Thanks again Mr./Ms._____, and have a wonderful _____.

TELEPHONE SCRIPT
For <u>MONTHLY</u> "B" & "C" PROSPECTS
FOLLOW-UP CALL

Hello Mr./Ms. _____, this is _____

from _____. I am calling simply as

a courtesy to keep in touch with you directly.

My intent is simply to ensure that I am doing all
that I can for you

at any given moment.

Its likely that since we last communicated you may
have arrived at

a point in the process where you feel ready to get
together for a no

obligation consultation.

O.K. I only ask because these consultations are
excellent sources

of information. Regardless of whether you're ready
to buy or sell

just yet these consultations offer an excellent opportunity to get

ACCURATE real estate and finance information. They can

answer those questions you may not even be aware you have.

What is the next available convenient time and day for you; would

you be available tomorrow?

(IF **YES** TO APPOINTMENT)
Excellent, I will certainly look forward to seeing you then. I have a market report relevant to your home you may find very interesting.

(IF **NO** TO AN APPOINTMENT)
That's fine. What I will do in the mean time is note that I did speak

with you and all is well. I will continue to keep you updated on the market via email periodically.

*Thanks again Mr./Ms._____, and
have a wonderful _____.*

CUSTOMER SERVICE HELPFUL TIPS

- Before you begin the day, remind yourself....

- Your task is to be the best possible agent to serve the needs of each new client.

- Customer service means NEVER having to say: "I'm sorry".

- Be POSITIVE ALWAYS
- Focus on what you do, not what you can't do
- You are the clients' FIRST contact; that is very important.
- You're not JUST a Realtor®; you are A CLIENT CARE REPRESENTATIVE! Be proud, talk proud!

ANSWERING THE CALL:

Take a deep breath.....

Look up, and smile....

Speak: ***Thank you for calling***

_____. ***How may I***
assist you?

End the call: ***I am looking forward to serving you***
further. Thank you for calling

_____.

PROBLEM CALLER SAMPLES
AND SUGGESTED RESPONSE

"I do not want to give you my name"

CSR: It sounds as though you have had a problem with giving your name to a Realtor® before. My objective in getting your name is to make certain that your real estate needs will be met. That process can begin with just a few short answers. May I get your name?

(If the caller identifies that he/she will not give a name because he/she does not want to be "hounded by a Realtor®", provide him/her with the assurance that he/she will ONLY be contacted based on the permission THEY give you.)

"I am just gathering information, or calling for a friend, or calling for a relative".

CSR: I can appreciate that. Are you going to be involved in the buying decision or participate in the purchase? [IF NO] - Often, the house that you call about does not fit your friend's need. A qualified agent can make your friend aware of other similar properties that may suit his/her needs. Can you see how getting that information directly from an agent would be advantageous? Could I get your name?

"I want the address so I can drive by and take a look at it."

CSR: Since you are going to invest the time to drive by, wouldn't it be worth your while to see the most charming part of the house? I could arrange to meet you, provide you all the particulars about the house and then take you to see the entire home in a personal showing. Could I get your name?

THE CALLER IS OBSTINANT ABOUT NOT PROVIDING A NAME

CSR: This puts us in a very awkward position. As you know, we have a fiduciary (trust) relationship with the Seller that prohibits us from giving out information to individuals who are unwilling to identify themselves. I am sure you understand the security and trust issues involved here and would expect the same courtesy if you were in the Seller's position.

"I already have an agent."

CSR: That's excellent. Would you mind giving me your agent's name and Company name? That will enable me to follow-up with him/her with additional information on other homes in this same area and price range that may be of interest to you.

C.R.M.
Client Relationship Management
Call Log Key

Rely upon the following key to ensure accurate use of the Call Log Sheet.

Primary Contact – Name (first & last) of the primary warm contact.

Secondary Contact – Name (first & last) of the secondary household individual such as a spouse.

Tel – Home telephone number. If primary number is cell, or other, indicate such.

Result – Indicate the call result; i.e. LM (Left Message), PNH (Primary Not Home), Good (spoke to), etc.

Refs – Always be mindful of the number of referrals to date. Indicate that number here.

Call Notes – Brief points of interest you may refer back to for the following month's call.

* Number of New Contacts Added this month? – Keep your W.C.L. (Warm Contact List) database up to date; keep track of new additions.

Set up Your Call Log: In spreadsheet format (MS Excel), create the following column headings.

1. **Primary Contact**
2. **Secondary Contact**
3. **Telephone**
4. **Result**
5. **Referrals**
6. **Call Notes**

MAPPING YOUR S.O.I.

WHO	NAME	EMAIL
Accountant		
Alhambra water guy		
Animal babysitter		
Athletic trainer		
Avon lady		
Babysitter		
Bakery		
Bank teller		
Barber		
Baseball coach		
Basketball coach		
Bicycle mechanic		
Boy/Girl Scouts' parents		
Brother-in-law		
Brothers of your 2 best friends		
Butcher		
Car detailer		
Caretaker		
Carpet Cleaner		
Checker at grocery store		
Child's teacher		
Church choir		
College professors		
Crossing guard		
Current co-workers		
Dentist		

Doctor
Drugstore worker
Dry Cleaner
Everyone in your dance class
your high school re-union list
High School friends
Eye doctor
Fed EX guy
Financial Planner
Fireman
Former boss
Former workmates
Friends at the gym
Friends from clubs
Gardner
Gas station owner
Grocer
Guy at the hardware store
Guy at the tire store
Gymnastics teacher
Gynecologist
Hairdresser
Headhunter or recruiter
House cleaner
Insurance Agent
Janitor
Jewelry person
Lady at the library
Landlord
Lifeguard
Liquor store owner
Local bartender
Local restaurant

Metro bus driver
Music teacher
Neighbor to you right
Neighbor to your left
Nurse
Owner of the fruit stand
Parents of your 2 best friends
Parents of your child's friends
Parents on your child's sports team
Parole Officer
Past co-workers
Pastor
People you meet at traffic school
Perfume person
Photo drive up
Police Officer
Postman
Pre-school teachers
Priest
Printer
Probation Officer
Receptionist at Dr. or Dentist
School bus driver
Sister-in-law
Sisters of your 2 best friends
Skiing buddies
Soccer coach
Softball coach
Someone that trained you
Sunday school teacher
Swimming teacher
Tailor
Tenants

Tennis teacher

The ice cream store owner

Therapist

Toastmasters

Travel Agent

UPS guy

Veterinarian

Video store owner

Who does your nails?

You oil change guy

Your child's art teacher

Your child's dentist

Your child's high school teacher

Your child's doctor

Your dance teacher

Your husband's boss

Your lawyer

Your mechanic

Your own high school teachers

Your wife's boss

This is a one year email campaign designed to build rapport with your databased prospects. Each message is "themed" based upon the month of the year and the campaign should be set in motion beginning with the corresponding month initiated.

Please feel free to modify the verbiage to suit your individual taste, manner of speaking, or preference. The bold caption beneath the month is meant to be the "subject" of the email. The campaign messages can certainly be used for content on snail mail mailouts as well; such as post cards, letters or other marketing materials.

JANUARY
Same Dreams, NEW Year!

Happy New Year! We all have unrealized dreams every year, that's the beauty of New Year's Day; we get another shot to honor our goals and dreams of the previous year.

I am not likely to be of any assistance to you regarding your personal fitness goals or your resolutions for improved health habits.

I'll tell you what though, many of us have real dreams of improving our standard of living:

- **A larger home**
- **Better neighborhood / better schools**
- **Lower mortgage payment**
- **A pool, or garden oasis – a real get-away backyard**
- **A newer car**
- **A well deserved dream vacation**

As your Realtor® of choice, I most certainly **CAN** assist you with all of the above! Contact me today, let's get started!

FEBRUARY
Happy Valentines Day!

February is so packed with holidays and special occasions. In addition to Valentines, there's President's Day, both Lincoln and Washington's birthdays, even Groundhog Day!

With so many, it just seems right to add one more, C.O.E., (Close of Escrow)! Why not? Contact me today, let's plot one VERY special day in February just for you!

MARCH
Bring in the Spring!

Wow! Spring is upon us and things are gearing up. No greater time for real estate buyers and sellers.

Give me a call today, let's discuss the value of your home and/or your wishes for that new home!

APRIL
Is it TAX Time Already?

Welcome to April, yes the tax season is upon us. Are you familiar with the many tax benefits to property ownership, even your mortgage payment?

Contact me today to schedule your no obligation consultation, in several ways real estate and taxes go hand in hand. Let's discuss some of them, let's talk about improving YOUR position.

MAY
Let's make May your month!

I am here to assist with any and all of your real estate needs.

Buying...... Selling, I can provide the answers you're looking for. Considering selling your home; allow me to provide you a Comparative Market Analysis and a free Summary Marketing Plan. Additionally, I can assist with cost of living data, community information, as well as ANY other consideration you may deem necessary to make your home purchase decision.

Memorial Day is always a great weekend for Sellers to show their homes and Buyers find it a wonderful weekend to get out and see what's on the market. In either case, let's make May your month!
Happy Mother's Day!

JUNE
A Father's Day to Remember.

Naturally, sellers want to receive top dollar for their home. Yet, in certain situations, you can increase the potential of closing a transaction by connecting with the seller relationally.

For example, let's say you find yourself competing for an original Frank Lloyd Wright designed home. After hearing about recent visit to Taliesin West, Wright's desert home, and your collection of Wright-inspired décor, the seller may be persuaded that you should be the next custodian of the property.

As I'm sure you can see, the relationship connection should be something more than simply a mutual affinity for gardening or Macintosh computing... Don't be afraid to involve your family in the Seller bonding process, after all June is the month of Father's Day and many Sellers can relate to your desire to provide a better home for your family.

Remember, sellers are just as emotionally connected to the home their selling as you are to the idea of buying it from them.

Call me today, and let's talk about increasing your potential to get the home of your dreams; Happy Father's Day!

JULY
Hotter Than July!

Did you see a "For Sale" sign that caught your attention? Perhaps a house in a neighborhood you've wanted to move into for some time? The ideal scenario would be to buy and sell simultaneously, but unfortunately, this is often not reality.

Buying a home first can be advantageous, especially if the home is truly your dream home. But, to get the property you want, you will probably have to leverage the equity in your existing home, or at least have an established target sale date.

On the other hand, you could end up with two houses. Bridge loans, or swing loans as they're sometimes called, can help with the down payment on your new home; but the stress of two mortgages can overwhelm even homeowners with very healthy incomes. Of course, if your home doesn't sell, then you do have the option of renting it out.

Either way, these Summer months are typically prime time for Buyers and Sellers and no more so than July.

The Independence Day weekend is pivotal for the real estate market. There are several things to consider. But, there's no need to go it alone, give me a call anytime to discuss the options.

AUGUST
Nearing the Fall Market

August somewhat rounds out the market for the Summer. No greater time to be planning the perfect Thanksgiving dinner served to family and friends in the home of your dreams!

Contact me today and let's get the process underway. I would be pleased to forward you MLS property listings via email. Take a good look at all the current market has to offer. Let me know which homes interest you and we will arrange a first-hand tour immediately.

If you've been contemplating selling your home, now's the time! Contact me for your no obligation

Consultation and I will show you how my expertise, backed with the POWER of our system can achieve the quickest positive result for you and your family.

SEPTEMBER
It's a Labor of Love!

Happy Labor Day all! What a wonderful time of the year! We can expect somewhat cooler temperatures as we leave summer behind and welcome the fall. Lot's of barbecues, picnics, and plenty of open houses!

If you've been considering selling your home, I am prepared to answer ALL of your questions to begin the process. Let's begin with a no obligation, in-home Consultation to discuss your home's market value and how the POWER of our marketing system can best be put into affect to sell your home.

Buyers never have a shortage of questions and I am always pleased to respond. Contact me today to schedule your no obligation Consultation and get the answers to your most pressing questions.

OCTOBER
Discover the world that awaits you!

October is the month of discovery! After all, it does bring us Columbus Day! Contact me today to schedule your in-home, no obligation Consultation and discover the world of real estate professionalism that is my commitment to you. Allow me to help you discover a new world; your new home!

I am YOUR Realtor® for life!

NOVEMBER
Be Ever Thankful!

Ah, the month of thanks giving! I want to take a moment to thank you for allowing me into your inbox here. It may sound corny but each message allows the opportunity for me to help you achieve your real estate or finance related goals and dreams.

Let's take it one step further; contact me today to schedule a no obligation Consultation to briefly discuss how making a buying or selling decision right now can truly open up a world where you have even MORE to be thankful for!

I am your Realtor® for life, and I am here to assist with all of your real estate and finance needs. Have a delightful Thanksgiving!

DECEMBER
The Most Wonderful Opportunity!

Make this December truly the most wonderful time of the year! Think back to perhaps a goal you set, or even a January resolution you made. Was it real estate of finance related, was it fulfilled? Will you be enjoying this holiday season from the comfort of the home of your dreams?

It's not too late! Contact me today to schedule your no obligation Consultation. Allow me just 15 minutes to show you how you can close out this year in the best possible way achieving your ultimate real estate goals and dreams!

Weekly Activities Plan
Maintain & Sustain

The "A", "B", "C"s of Prospecting is much more than a single session learning experience. For every Real Estate Sales Professional, this system is the ultimate productivity platform from which you can literally run and grow your business. It enables you to utilize many activities and protocols for the everyday vital tasks that we associate with being a successful Real Estate Sales professional.

In this regard, this Weekly Activities Detail encompasses recommended practical applications for the system tasks and tools. If you take this Weekly Activities Detail to heart and apply it diligently, we are confident that you will find substantially increased efficiency, timeliness and productivity with regard to your own career efforts.

Important to remember, the tasks and schedule set forth below are not necessarily designed to be implemented with rigidity, but rather to provide you a conceptual usage plan. It is recommended that you conduct each of the following activities, but you will no doubt develop a daily routine comfortable for you.

DAY	ACTIVITY
Monday	**Database Management:** • Enter contacts into your database – Prospects, SOI, past clients, etc • Be certain to appropriately categorize contacts
Tuesday	• Manage Calendar / Plot office events, training, birthdays, client anniversary dates, etc. on your personal calendar and check it for any newly added Branch or Company events.
Wednesday	**Prospecting:** • Manage Campaigns / Create, structure and send out marketing (CRM) campaigns via email for your contact categories and marketing groups. (Your Prospects, SOI, Buyers, Sellers, past clients, etc.) • Send out "JUST LISTED/SOLD" announcements; (snail mail & email)
Thursday	• Leads Management /Review status and follow-up necessity for all new and existing leads. Know their temperature.

Friday	**Website & Marketing Plan Check:**
	• Review your marketing plan – Is it inline with your current activities?
	• Check your website, conduct site maintenance, and observations.
	• Ask yourself; am I doing ALL that I can to promote my web address?
	• What kind of traffic am I getting, what can I do to drive MORE?
	• Is ANY content on my site dated, in need of deletion or updating?
	• Analyze the return/effectiveness of each element of your marketing plan.
	• Is each marketing expense justifiable? Can I add or substitute actions?

You are further encouraged to assess daily, your overall utilization of the "A", "B", "C"s of Prospecting system. **It is truly everything, every Real Estate Sales Professional needs to succeed!**

Lesson Notes:

Lesson Notes:

Lesson Notes:

Lesson Notes

Lesson Notes

Lesson Notes

Lesson Notes

New Contacts for Data Entry

--

--

--

--

--

--

--

--

--

--

--

--

--

--

--

--

--

--

--

--

--

--

--

--

--

--

--

New Contacts for Data Entry

--

--

--

--

--

--

--

--

--

--

--

--

--

--

New Contacts for Data Entry

--

--

--

--

--

--

--

--

--

--

--

--

--

--